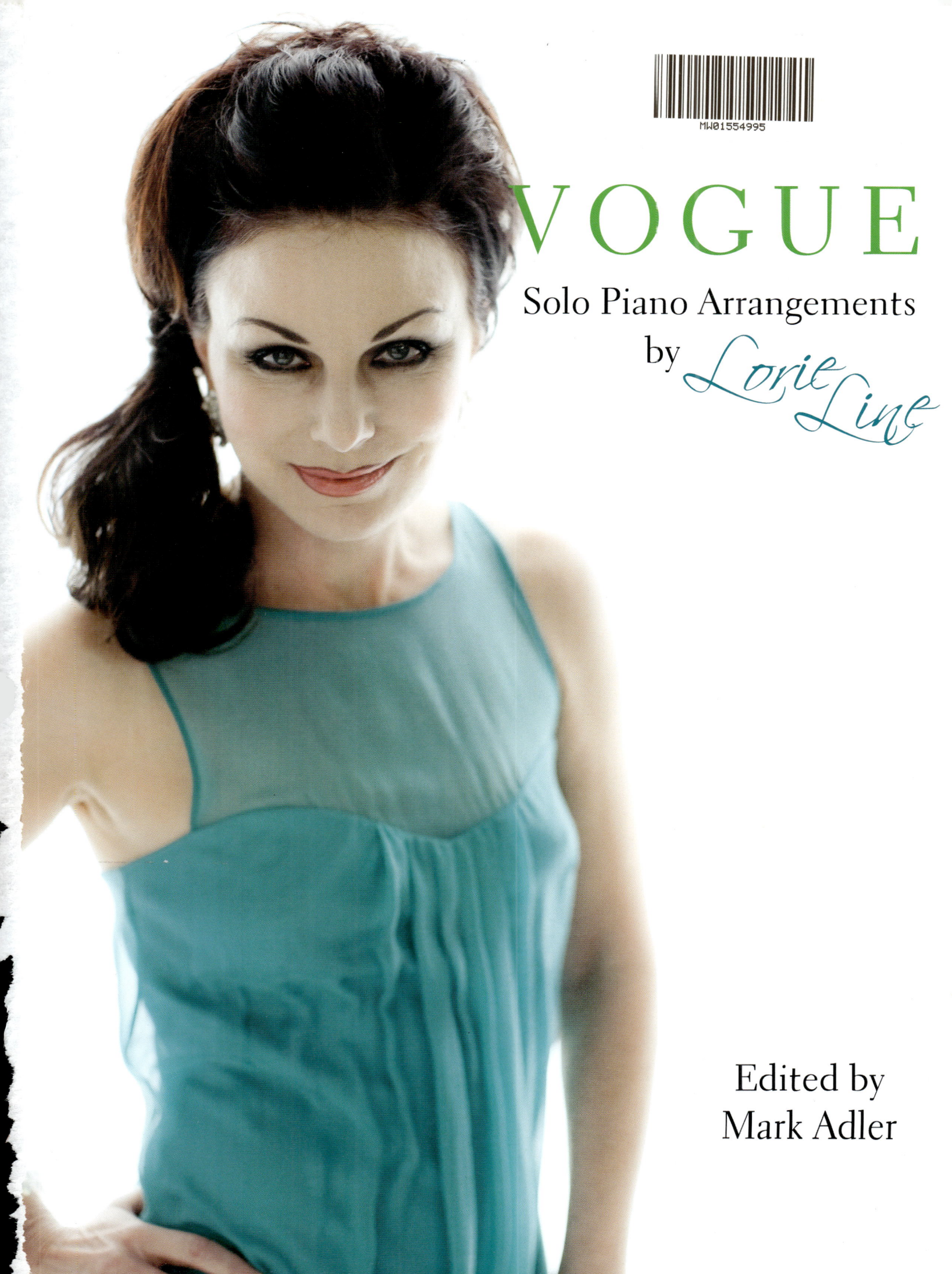

MANAGED AND DISTRIBUTED BY

Lorie Line Music, Inc.
222 Minnetonka Avenue South
Wayzata, MN 55391
1.800.801.5463 (LINE)

RECORDING NOTES

Recorded at Studio L on Lake Minnetonka on Esmeralda, Lorie's personal Yamaha CFIIIS concert grand piano

CREDITS

Produced by • Lorie Line
All music arranged and orchestrated by • Lorie Line
Piano Technician • Mark Barnier
Audio Engineer • Scott Miller
Mixed by • Lorie Line and Scott Miller
Photography • Joel Larson
Hair • Amy Wagner
Graphic Design • Kris Braaten and Wendy Griak

FOR TOUR SCHEDULE
AND MORE INFORMATION
www.lorieline.com

TABLE OF CONTENTS

●●● **I MISS THE MOUNTAINS** 5
from the Broadway musical *Next To Normal*

●● **FEED THE BIRDS (TUPPENCE A BAG)** 11
from the Broadway musical *Mary Poppins*

●● **LOVE STORY** 18
by *Taylor Swift*

●● **INTO THE WEST** 24
from the movie *Lord Of The Rings*

●●● **AS LONG AS YOU'RE MINE** 31
from the Broadway musical *Wicked*

●●● **FAITHFULLY** 38
from the hit TV series *GLEE*

●● **LEANING ON THE EVERLASTING ARMS** 46
traditional hymn featured in the movie *True Grit*

●● **I SEE THE LIGHT** 54
from Walt Disney's movie *Tangled*

● **I GOTTA FEELING** 60
by *The Black Eyed Peas*

●● **BIG BRIGHT BEAUTIFUL WORLD (REPRISE)** 70
from the Broadway musical *Shrek*
CELLO ACCOMPANIMENT 75

● **THE KING'S SPEECH** 76
from the movie *The King's Speech*
CELLO ACCOMPANIMENT 80

●●● **I SEE YOU** 82
from the movie *Avatar*

BEGINNERS SHOULD START WITH SONGS MARKED WITH A SINGLE DOT (●).
INTERMEDIATE PLAYERS WILL ENJOY PLAYING MUSIC MARKED WITH A DOUBLE DOT (●●).
ADVANCED READERS AND PLAYERS CAN PLAY ALL THE MUSIC IN THIS BOOK AND MUSIC WITH THREE DOTS (●●●).

Contains all the music as played on the CD except *Hedwig's Theme* as we were not able to obtain publishing rights.

ABOUT THE PROJECT

Dear Fans,

The music on this album is the latest and greatest for 2011. I called it VOGUE because it is the most fashionable music of the day. Many of the songs were so new that at the time of this recording, some tunes weren't even published and I had to learn them totally by ear. That was really fun! A couple of them are older, but brand new to a new fan base. I grew up with *Faithfully*, but it was Journey that made it famous. And then, *Feed The Birds* has always been my favorite Mary Poppins song since childhood, but just recently it was reborn with a brand new play on Broadway. And, last but certainly not least, *Leaning On The Everlasting Arms* was one of the first songs I ever learned at the Church of Christ in Sparks, Nevada. This song reignited as the theme song for True Grit this year and when I went to see the movie, I found myself singing along. I still remember every word.

I recorded a few songs that are popular with the "younger" audience, and I hope my more mature fans will appreciate and enjoy my arrangements of such hip artists and groups like *Taylor Swift* and *The Black Eyed Peas*. Wow, they've got it going on. I also hope my budding pianists (who follow me) will enjoy playing these arrangements. Hopefully you will be encouraged to keep practicing!

It is hard to believe, but I've been in this business now for over 20 years. I still love to try new music, even if it is techno, pop or rock n' roll, all the while putting my signature "Lorie Line" touch on whatever I do. I think it keeps me young. It keeps me thinking, reflecting, learning, feeling, dreaming, and of course praising God who has made all things possible and beautiful for me.

Thank you for being my fans. Enjoy the music.

Lorie Line

MUSICIANS ON THE ALBUM

PIANO • Lorie Line
KEYBOARDS, SYNTHESIZER
(strings, horn, accordion, glockenspiel, bells, music box, electric piano, bassoon, voices)
GUITARS • Dean Magraw
ELECTRIC GUITAR • David Young
(*Faithfully* and *Hedwig's Theme*)
BANJO • Brian Fesler
HARMONICA • Bruce Kurnow
OBOE • Merilee Klemp
WOODWINDS • Kenni Holmen
NATIVE AMERICAN FLUTE
CELLO • Kirsten Whitson
ACOUSTIC BASS • Gordy Johnson
(electric on *As Long As You're Mine*)
ELECTRIC and ARCO BASS • Ian Allison
DRUMS • Nate Babbs

I Miss The Mountains

(from the Broadway musical Next To Normal)

Lyrics by Brian Yorkey
Music by Tom Kitt

Arranged by Lorie Line

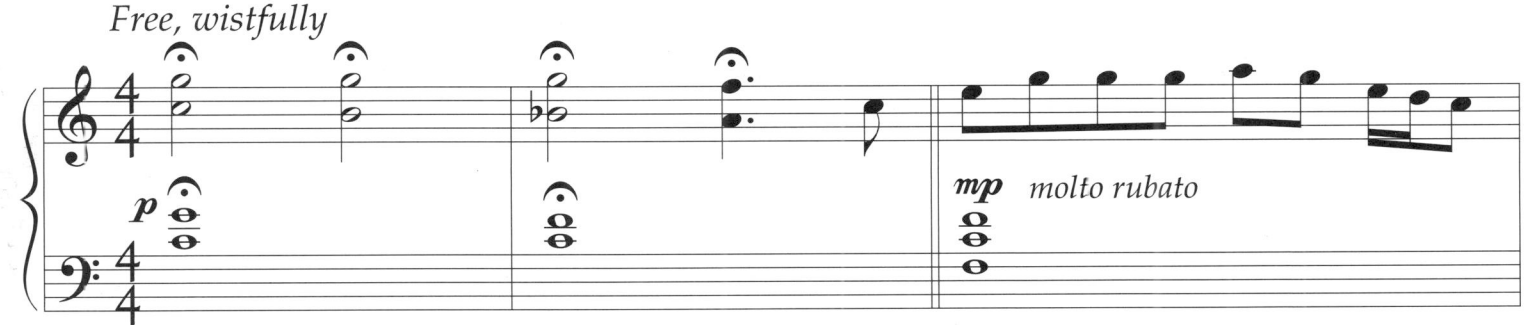

©2009 LONELY SATELLITE MUSIC (BMI) AND TOM KITT MUSIC (BMI)
All Rights Administered by WARNER-TAMERLANE PUBLISHING CORP. (BMI)
This Arrangement © 2011 LONELY SATELLITE MUSIC (BMI) AND TOM KITT MUSIC (BMI)
All Rights Reserved.
Used by Permission of ALFRED PUBLISHING CO., INC.

Feed The Birds (Tuppence A Bag)
(from Walt Disney's Mary Poppins)

Words and Music by
Richard M. Sherman and Robert B. Sherman

Arranged by Lorie Line

Love Story

Words and Music by Taylor Swift *Arranged by Lorie Line*

Strictly in time ♩ = 120

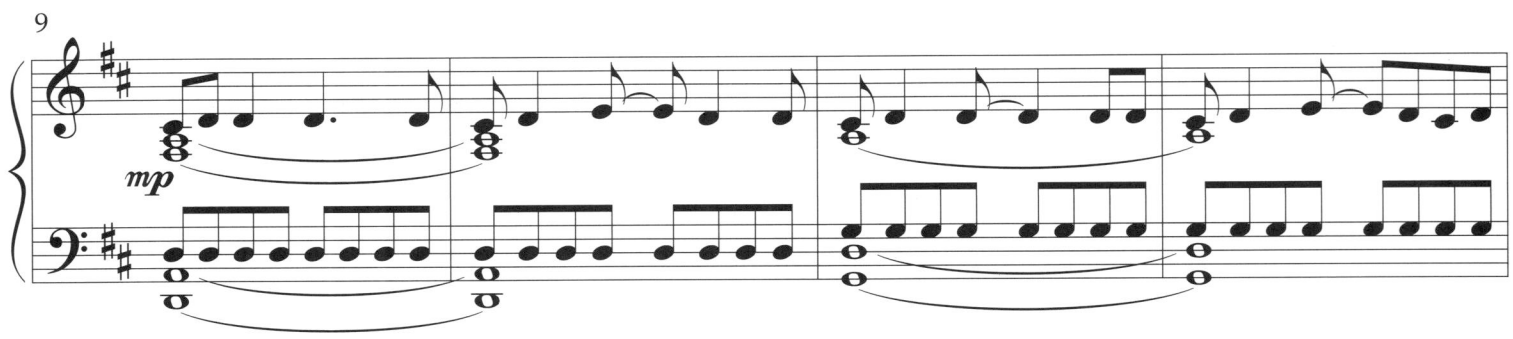

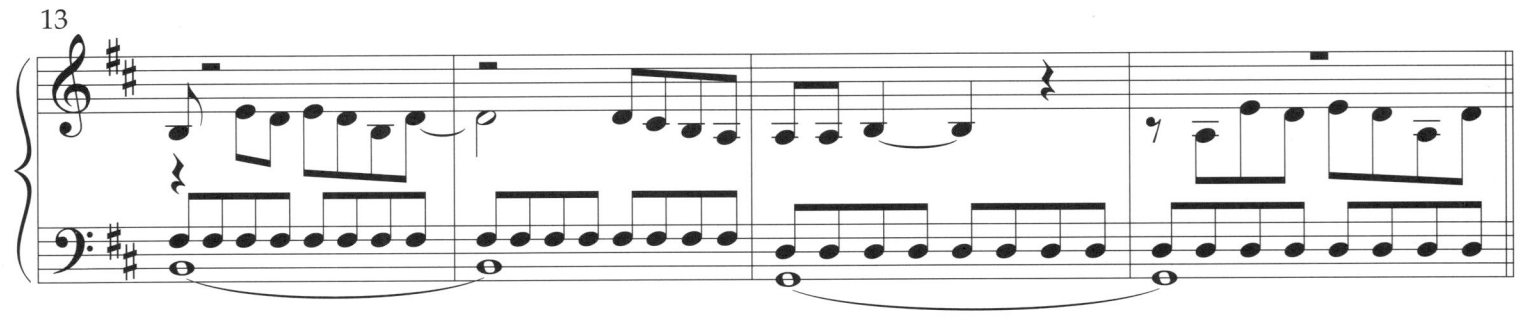

Copyright © 2008 Sony/ATV Music Publishing LLC and Taylor Swift Music
This arrangement Copyright © 2011 Sony/ATV Music Publishing LLC and Taylor Swift Music
All Rights Administered by Sony/ATV Music Publishing LLC, 8 Music Square West, Nashville, TN 37203
International Copyright Secured. All Rights Reserved.

Into The West

(from The Lord Of The Rings; The Return Of The King)

Words and Music by
Annie Lennox, Howard Shore and Fran Walsh

Arranged by Lorie Line

Copyright © 2003 by La Lennoxa Ltd., New Line Tunes and South Fifth Avenue Publishing
This arrangement Copyright © 2011 by La Lennoxa Ltd., New Line Tunes and South Fifth Avenue Publishing
All Rights for La Lennoxa Ltd. for the World Administered by Universal MGB Music Publishing Ltd.
All Rights for Universal MGB Music Publishing Ltd. in the U.S. Administered by Universal Music - MGB Songs
International Copyright Secured. All Rights Reserved.

As Long As You're Mine
(from the Broadway musical Wicked)

Music and Lyrics by Stephen Schwartz Arranged by Lorie Line

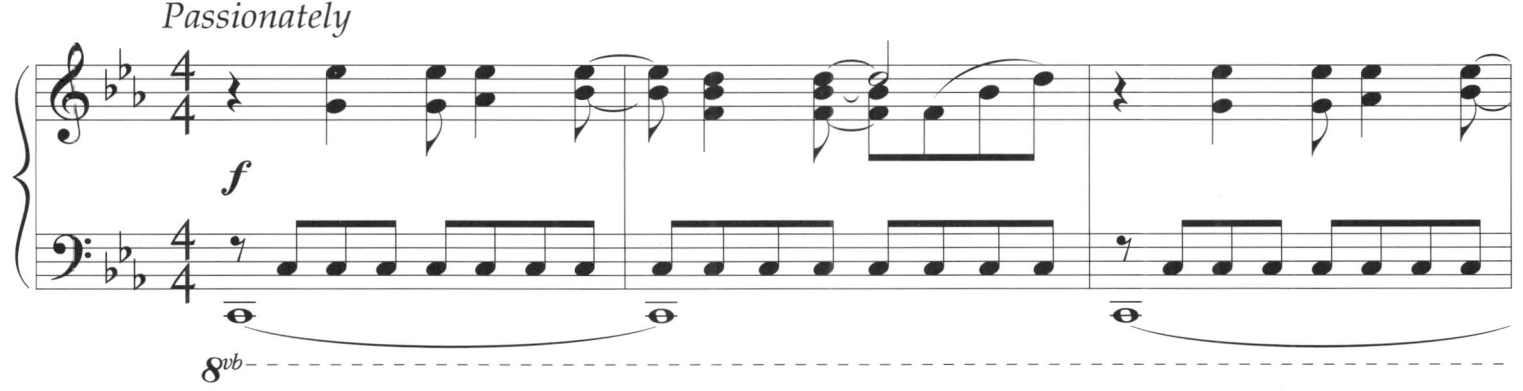

Copyright © 2003 Greydog Music
This arrangement Copyright © 2011 Greydog Music
All Rights Reserved. Used By Permission.

31

Faithfully
(from the hit TV series GLEE)

Words and Music by Jonathan Cain *Arranged by Lorie Line*

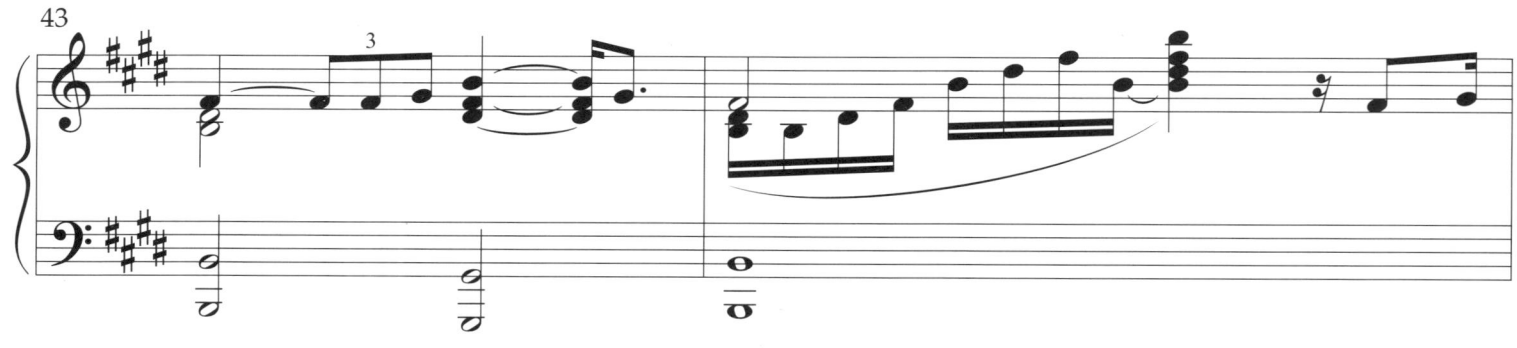

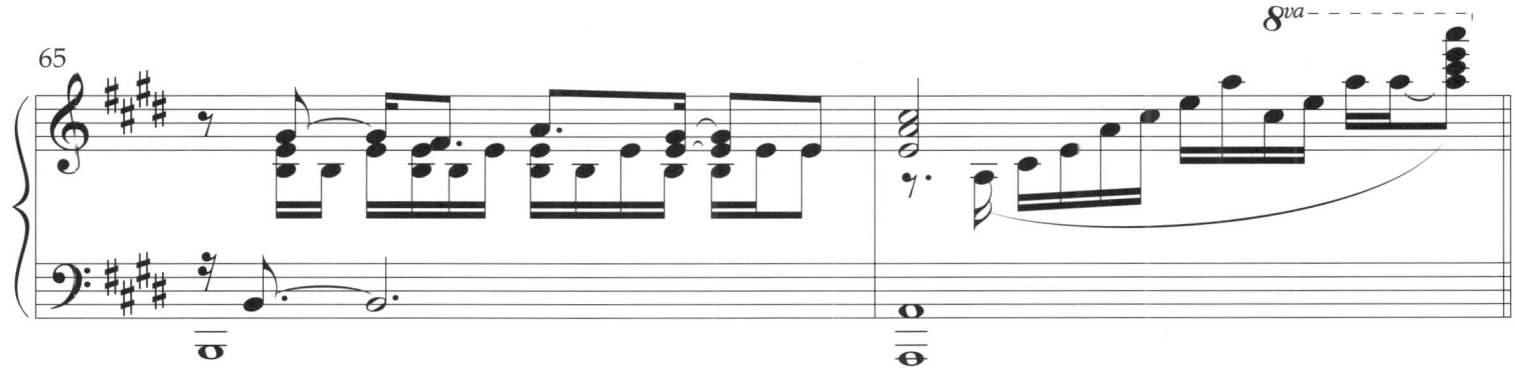

Leaning On The Everlasting Arms
(traditional hymn featured in the movie True Grit)

Traditional   Arranged by Lorie Line

Copyright © 2011 Lorie Line Music, Inc.
222 Minnetonka Avenue South
Wayzata, Minnesota
All Rights Reserved

I See The Light
(from Walt Disney's movie Tangled)

Music by Alan Menken
Lyrics by Glenn Slater

Arranged by Lorie Line

© 2010 Wonderland Music Company, Inc. and Walt Disney Music Company

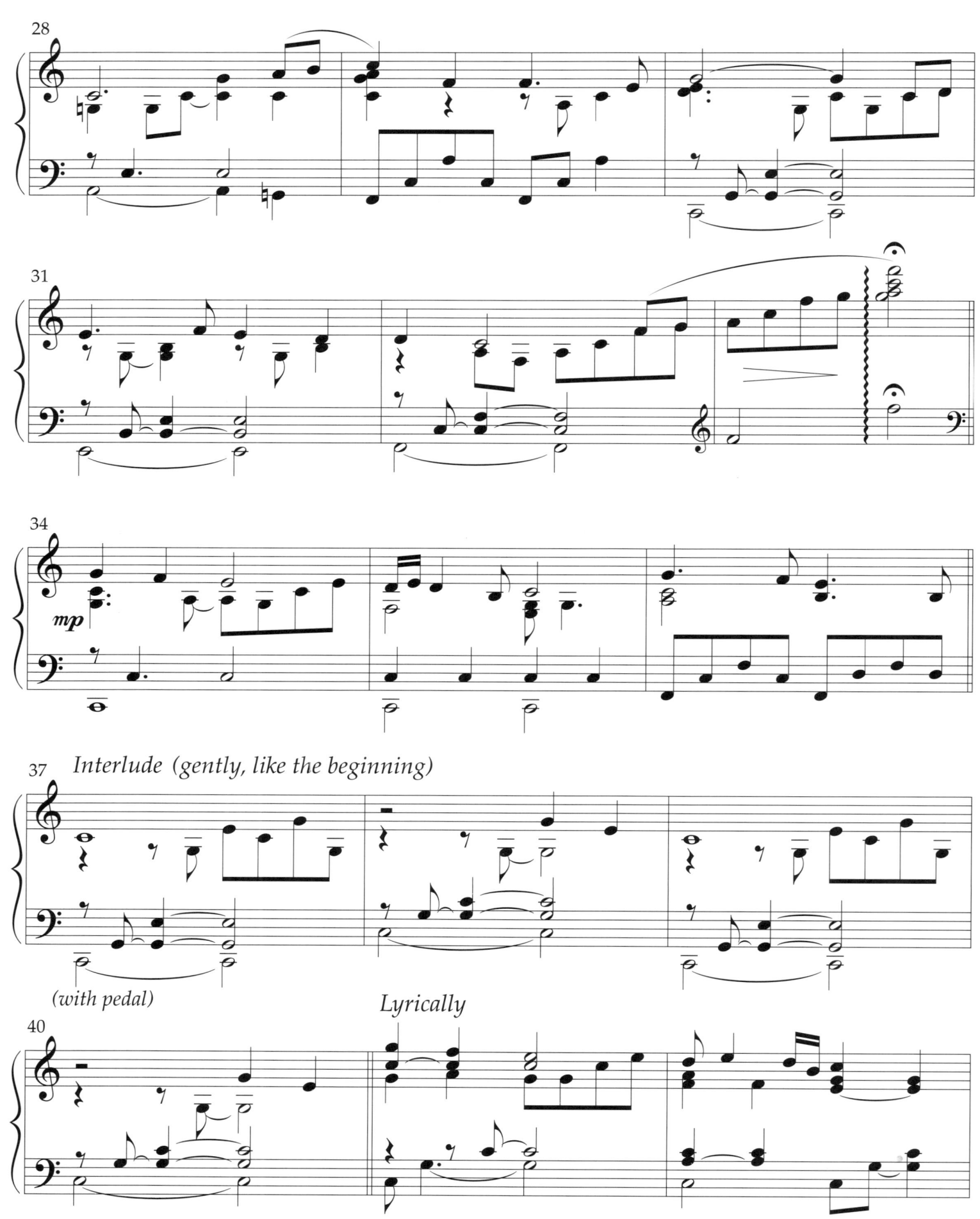

I Gotta Feeling

Words and Music by
Will Adams, Allan Pineda, Jaime Gomez,
Stacy Ferguson, David Guetta and Frederic Riesterer

Arranged by Lorie Line

Copyright © 2009 BMG Sapphire Songs (BMI), Will.I.Am Music Inc. (BMI), Jeepney Music Publishing (BMI), Tab Magnetic Publishing (BMI),
EMI April Music Inc. (ASCAP), Headphone Junkie Publishing (ASCAP), Square Rivoli Publishing (SACEM) and Rister Editions (SACEM)
This arrangement Copyright © 2011 BMG Sapphire Songs (BMI), Will.I.Am Music Inc. (BMI), Jeepney Music Publishing (BMI), Tab Magnetic Publishing (BMI),
EMI April Music Inc. (ASCAP), Headphone Junkie Publishing (ASCAP), Square Rivoli Publishing (SACEM) and Rister Editions (SACEM)
Worldwide Rights for Will.I.Am Music Inc., Jeepney Music Publishing and Tab Magnetic Publishing Administeredd by BMG Sapphire Songs
All Rights for Headphone Junkie Publishing Controlled and Administered by EMI April Music Inc.
All Rights for Square Rivoli Publishing and Rister Editions in the U.S. Administered by Shapiro, Bernstein & Co. Inc.
International Copyright Secured. All Rights Reserved.

Melody (with Fergie)

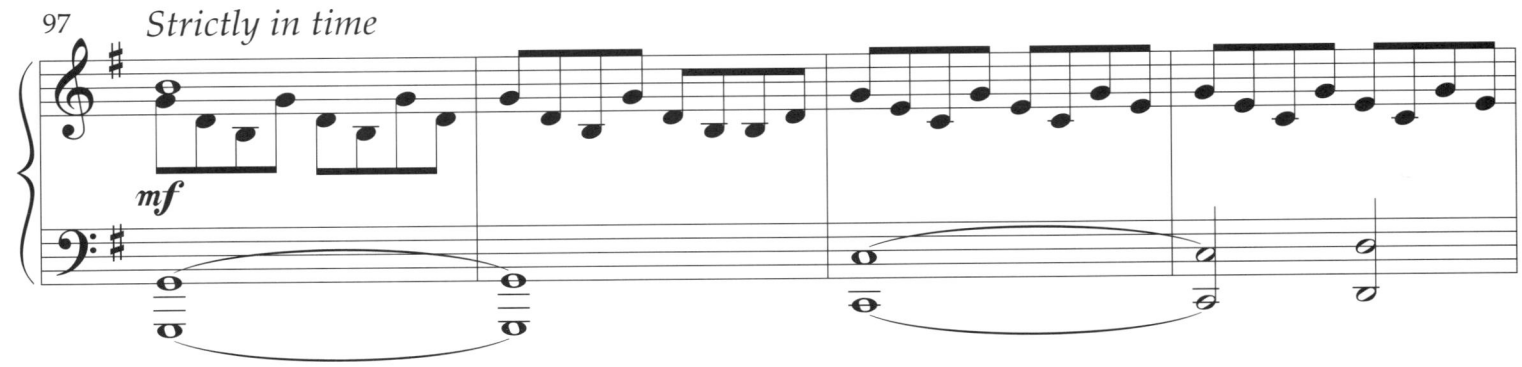
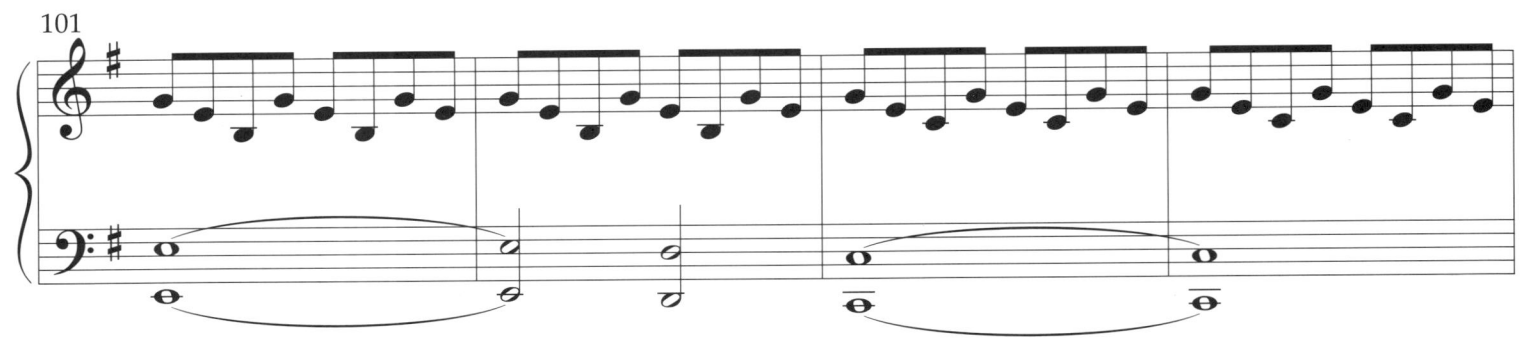
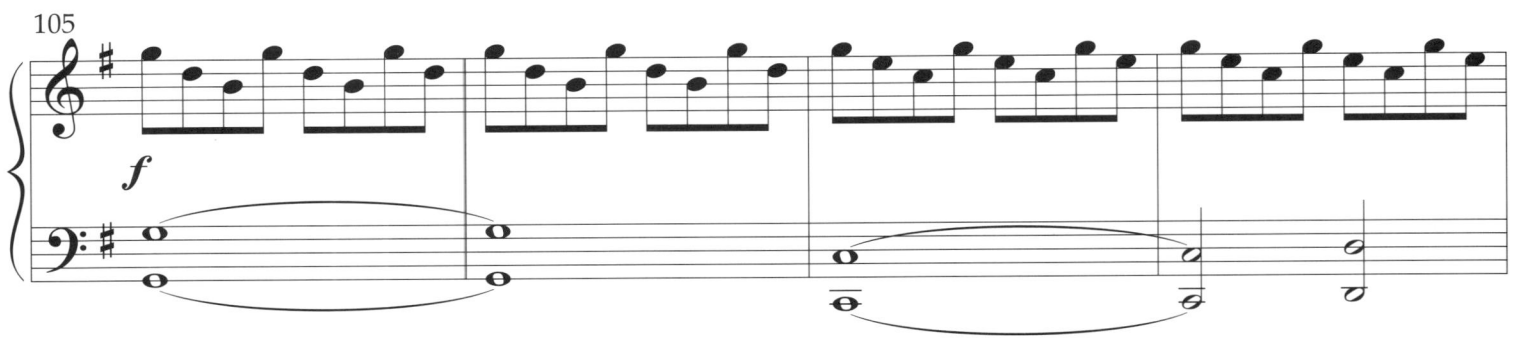
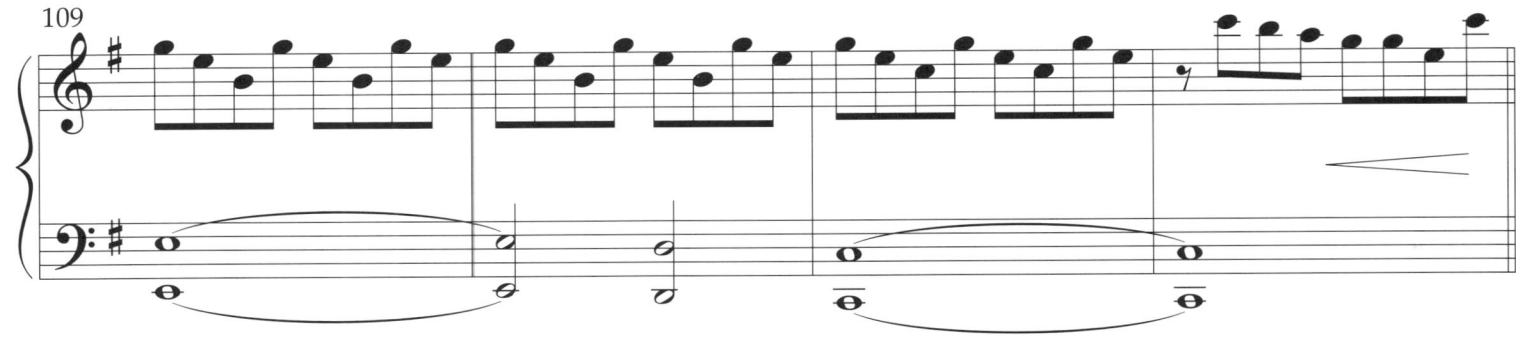

Big Bright Beautiful World
(Reprise) (from the Broadway musical Shrek)

Words by David Lindsay-Abaire
Music by Jeanine Tesori

Arranged by Lorie Line

Copyright ©2008 DWA Songs (ASCAP)
This arrangement Copyright © 2011 DWA Songs (ASCAP)
Worldwide Rights for DWA Songs Administered by BMG Ruby Songs
International Copyright Secured. All Rights Reserved.

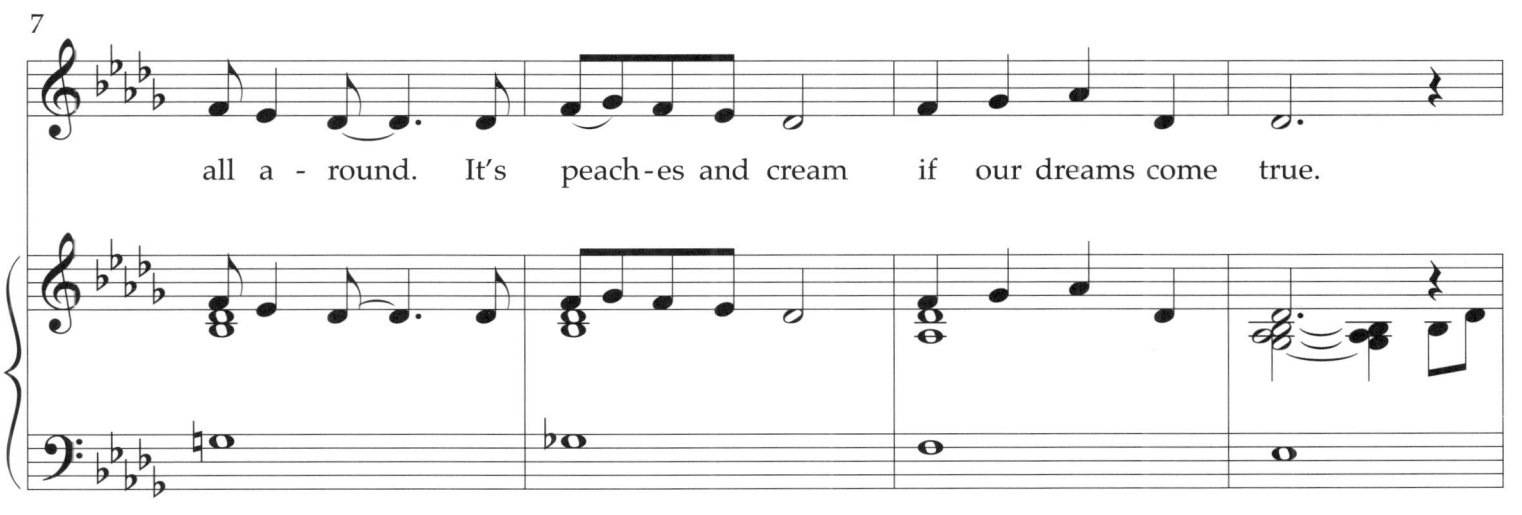

17
you won't mind the view. I
20
know I'm not the hand - some prince for whom you've wait - ed.
mf
23
I don't have a fan - cy cas - tle and I'm not so - phi - sti - ca - ted, a

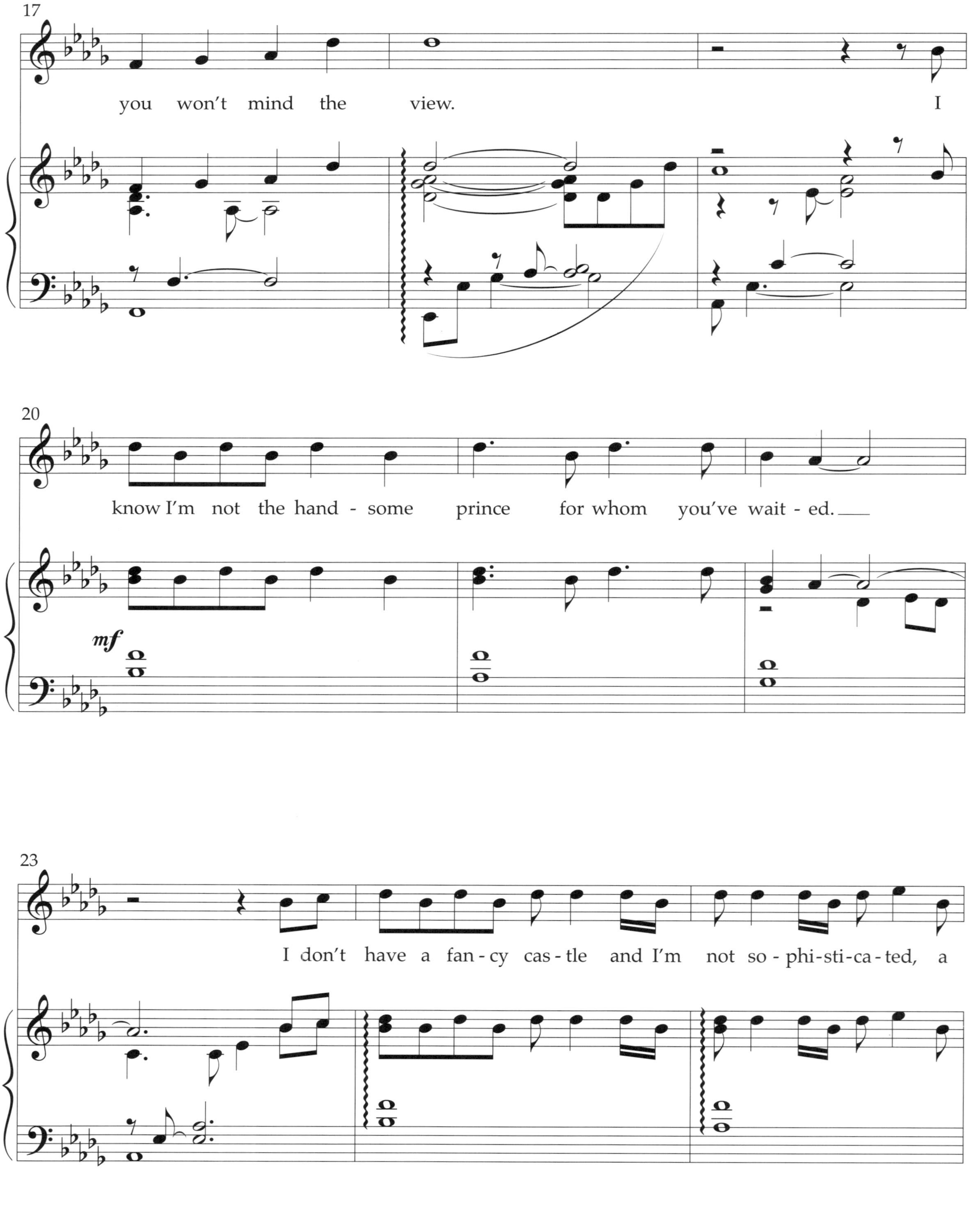

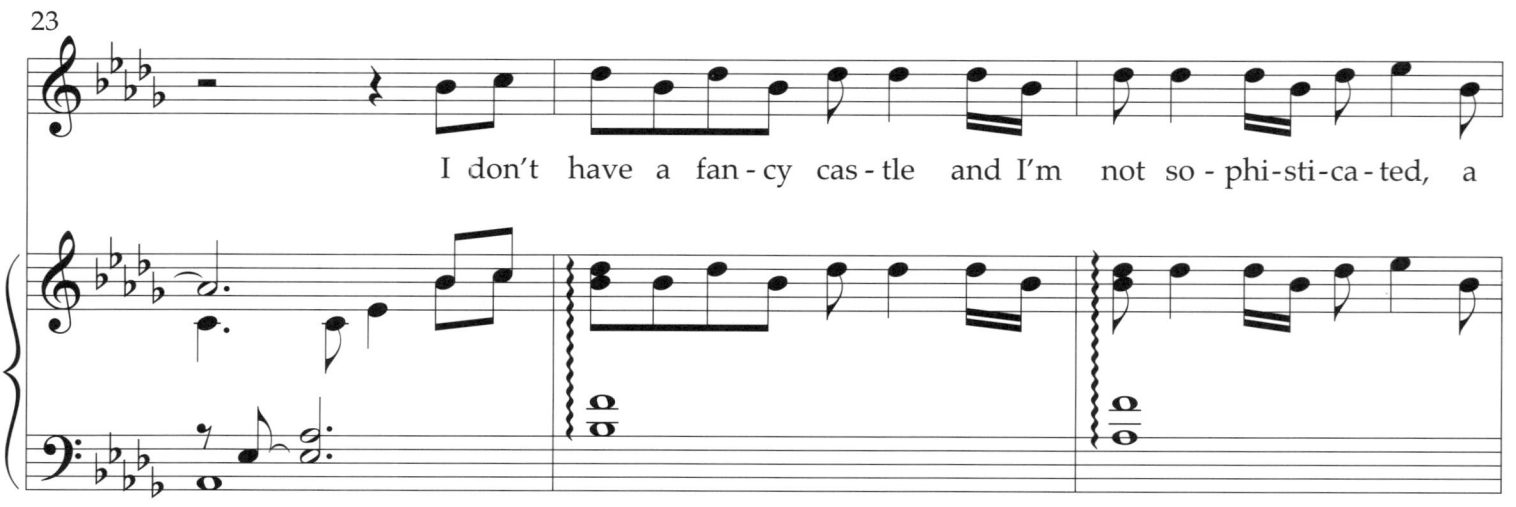

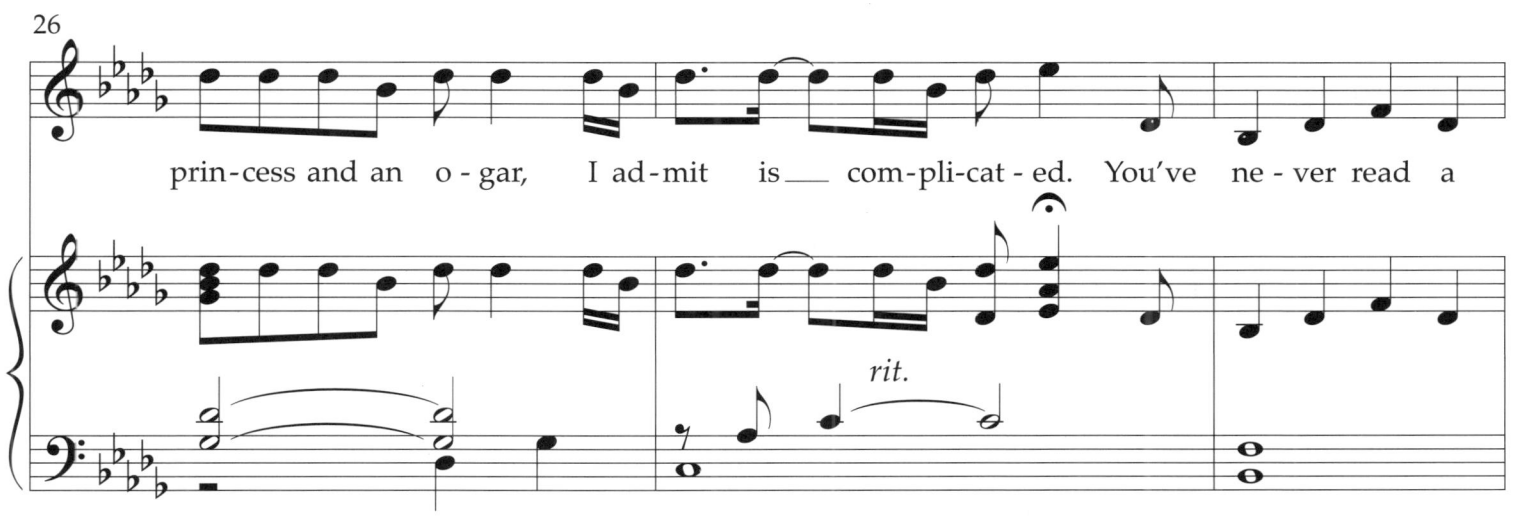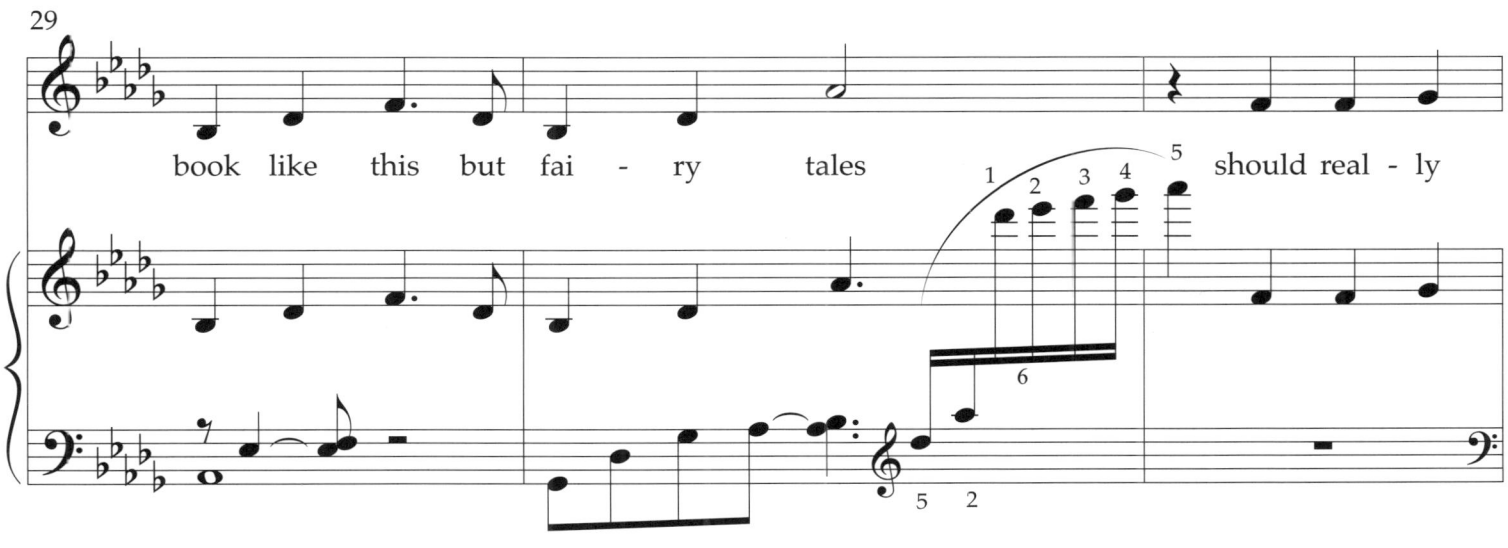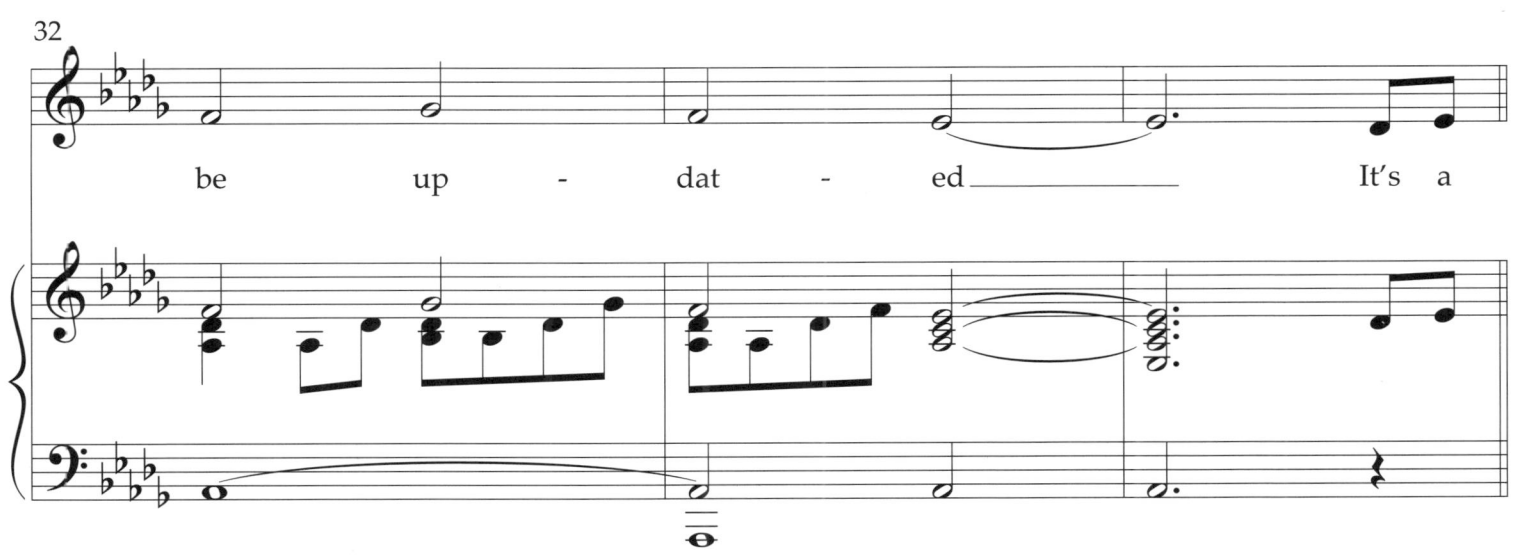

Big Bright Beautiful World

(Reprise) (from the Broadway musical Shrek)

Cello

Arranged by Lorie Line

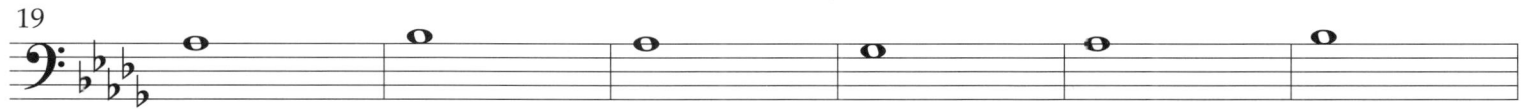

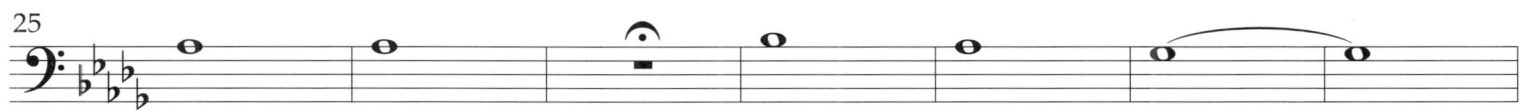

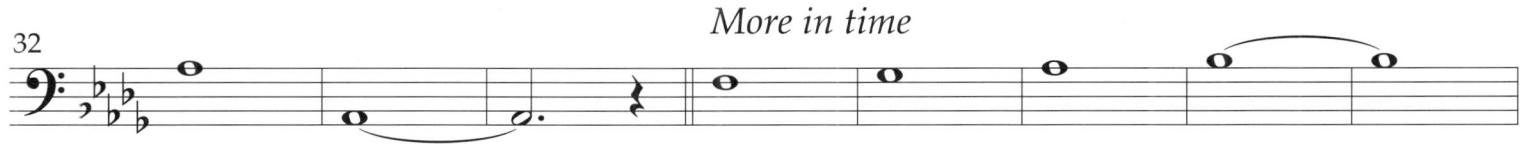

Copyright ©2008 DWA Songs (ASCAP)
This arrangement Copyright © 2011 DWA Songs (ASCAP)
Worldwide Rights for DWA Songs Administered by BMG Ruby Songs
International Copyright Secured. All Rights Reserved.

The King's Speech
(from the movie The King's Speech)

Written by Alexandre Desplat *Arranged by Lorie Line*

The King's Speech

(from the movie The King's Speech)

Arranged by Lorie Line

Cello

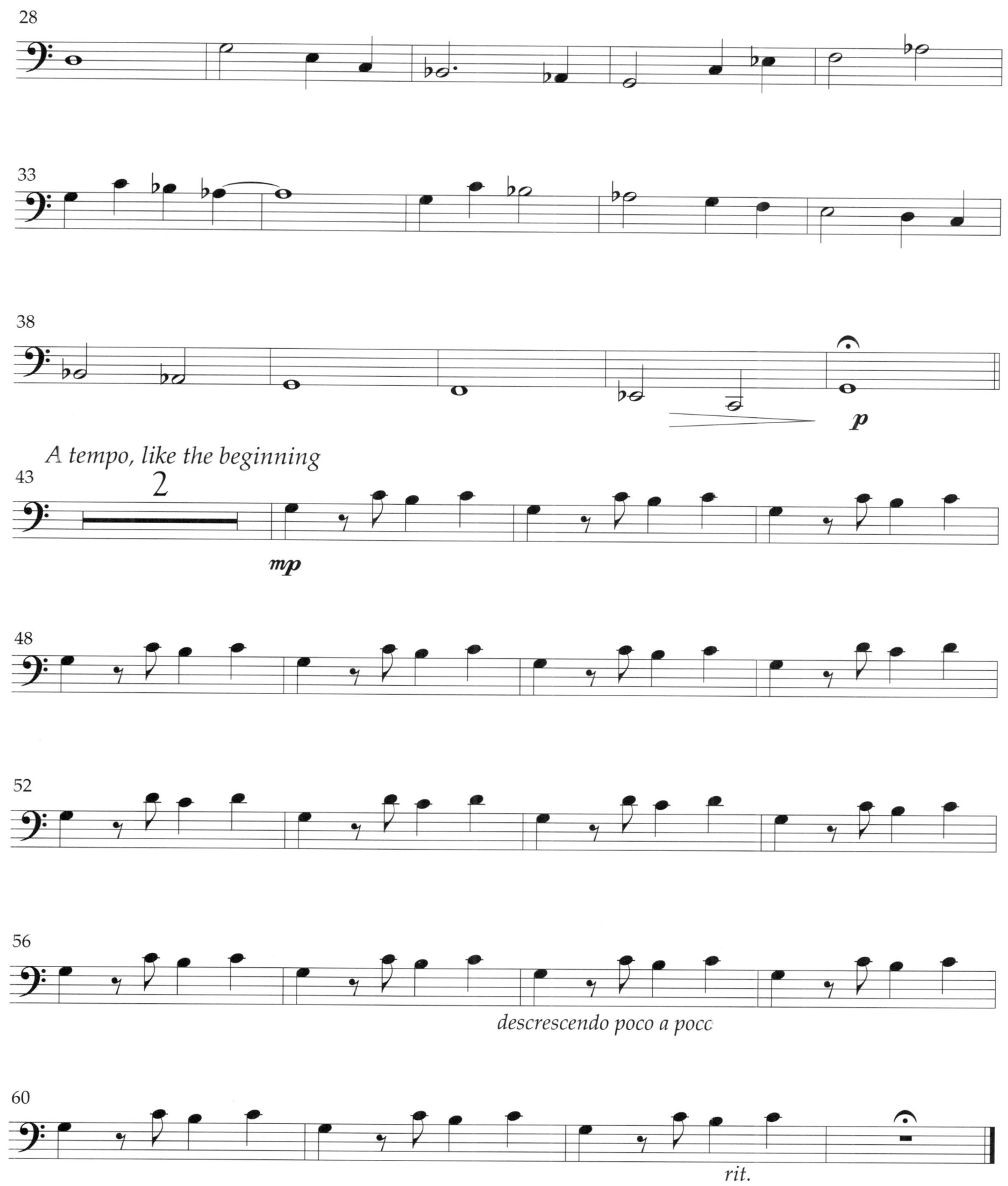

I See You
(from the movie Avatar)

Lyrics by Simon Franglen, James Horner and Kuk Harrell
Music by James Horner and Simon Franglen

Arranged by Lorie Line